BOOKS BY ALINE AMON

Reading, Writing, Chattering Chimps
Orangutan: Endangered Ape
Roadrunners and Other Cuckoos

Roadrunners and Other Cuckoos

Yellow-billed
Cuckoo

Roadrunner

Groove-billed
Ani

Squirrel
Cuckoo

Hoatzin

SOME NEW WORLD CUCKOOS

Coucal

WRITTEN & ILLUSTRATED BY

Aline Amon

Roadrunners and Other Cuckoos

ATHENEUM   NEW YORK   1978

European
Cuckoo

Red-faced
Malkoha

Emerald Cuckoo

SOME OLD WORLD CUCKOOS

For Florence Nielsen Goodrich

LIBRARY OF CONGRESS CATALOGING IN PUBLICATION DATA

Amon, Aline.
    Roadrunners and other cuckoos

    Bibliography: p. 82
    Includes index.
    SUMMARY: Discusses the physical characteristics and
behavior of species of the cuckoo family
found around the world.
    1. Cuckoos—Juvenile literature. [1. Cuckoos]
I. Title.
QL696.C83A46   598.7'4   78-6648
ISBN 0-689-30646-6

ACKNOWLEDGMENTS

I am indebted to Dr. John Farrand, Jr., of the Ornithology Department of the American Museum of Natural History, for his invaluable assistance in straightening out the confusions of classification and other cuckoo questions. He also checked the entire manuscript for accuracy with a meticulousness which I deeply appreciate.

This book, like those of many other authors, would not exist without the wealth of material available in the research branches of the New York Public Library, and in the collections of the Audubon Society and Natural History Museum Libraries.

Finally, I want to thank my family for their customary patience, and birding friends for their enthusiastic interest in cuckoos and the birds' odd, adaptive ways.

Contents

Roadrunner

Snake Birds

ROADRUNNERS

A hungry roadrunner strides across the sandy desert floor. She spies a rattlesnake.

The snake sees her, too. He coils his body and lifts his head. The horny segments of his tail scrape together. They rattle.

The roadrunner ignores the warning. She fluffs out her feathers and spreads her wings. Then she attacks, jabbing her long beak at the reptile. The snake's head shoots forward, mouth stretched wide. It closes harmlessly on a bunch of loose wing feathers. The rattler strikes again. More feathers.

All the time the roadrunner stabs the snake, hunting for weak spots. Then, she finds one. The reptile's tense coils relax. His head slides down onto the sand as he dies.

The bird swallows as much of the snake as she can.

He is young, but still too long. An inch of tail, and the silent rattle, hang from the roadrunner's bill. After part of her prey is digested, she will gulp down more until the meal is finished. Meanwhile she pays no attention to her overfull beak.

Bright eyes peer out under her ragged crest. They shoot glances at sand and stone, cactus and mesquite, searching for the best path to another victim.

Decided, she shakes her loose, brown-streaked feathers into place. Then she starts forward, but she does not fly. She lopes, instead, toward a jumble of rocks on the edge of a dry wash. There water runs only after the rare rains, short but violent. There, too, lizards and insects hide in cracks from the baking sun.

Her dark shadow races with the roadrunner—black crest bouncing, strong shadow legs moving like scissors, and long tail flicking up and down. It is as comical as the bird herself.

No wonder people have made up stories about road-runners: winged creatures that prefer to walk; animals of less than a pound that tackle the deadly snakes feared by humans.

One story explains the bird's immunity to venom. If bitten, it streaks in search of a certain herb, an antidote to the rattler's poison. Unfortunately for people, this magical plant seems to be the roadrunner's secret.

Another tale reveals how such a simple creature can handle a rattler. The clever bird is supposed to build a fence around any snake it finds asleep, a prickly fence of sharp twigs and cactus spines. When the drowsy reptile awakes, it tries to escape, without success. The rattler becomes so tired it gives up looking for a safe route and attacks the fence directly. It is caught on the spikes. In another version, the frustrated snake bites itself to death. Either way, it ends up in the stomach of the bird.

Despite this story, the only things roadrunners build are their nests. Before these are made, the males court their mates.

On a bright spring morning, one male greets the rising sun from atop a rock or stump. He dips his bill almost to his toes and starts a series of melancholy hoots, "Coo-coo-coo-ooh-ooh-ooh." With each hoarse note his head rises, until his beak points to the lightening sky. And with each note the call becomes deeper and throatier. Even a scientist has called this a "love song."

The roadrunner keeps performing for up to an hour. If there is a female watching, the male struts about, head high, short wings and long tail drooping. He stops for a moment to bow politely and then goes on with his parade.

Although roadrunners travel on the ground by choice, they often climb through the brush and can fly if they must. In spring, the birds build nests several feet high in cactus clumps or desert bushes. There the eggs and young will be safe. The nests are tangles of sticks, roots, feathers, leaves, flakes of dry manure—and the skins shed by growing snakes.

A roadrunner lays three to six chalky white eggs, but sometimes a nest is found with up to a dozen in it. The extra ones were laid by a second bird. Now and then a female chooses another's nest as a fine place for her own eggs. These rare, lazy roadrunners apparently never return to help the nesting mother raise the big brood.

The first eggs hatch earliest and the others follow. The busy parents must incubate the latecomers while also caring for hungry babies. The male and female take turns at brooding young and eggs and at finding food for their growing family. When the hunter brings home its prey, it is mobbed by eager chicks, buzzing in anticipation.

Many birds will pretend to be injured when their young are threatened. With a wing trailing as if broken, a parent staggers away from its nest. Predators are lured into following the "helpless" adult—and forgetting the undefended chicks. Far from its nest, the cripple recovers miraculously and flies back to its family with ease.

One roadrunner had the same intention, but it faked a broken leg rather than wing. The bird, apparently in terrible shape, squirmed across the sand. It pushed and dragged its body for thirty-five feet, often rolling over in the dust. The human intruder close to its nest was amused by the show, but he did not go after the desperate roadrunner. When the bird saw that its ruse was not working, it ran back the full thirty-five feet on two healthy legs. Then it started out again, limping. The struggling bird would have caught the attention of any hungry animal.

Even the observer admired its efforts so much that he finally followed the "broken-legged" actor, just as he was supposed to do.

Newly hatched roadrunners are black with bare faces that have been compared to those of reptiles. They are dressed only in thin white hairs which show where the feathers will grow later.

In one brood, real plumage began to appear rapidly by the first of May. Three days later, the young roadrunners were well clad, but they still had ridiculously short tails compared to those of the adults—a mere inch-and-a-half. Although they walked unsteadily, the time had come for them to leave the nest and discover the desert.

Roadrunners have some unusual habits which help them survive in the dry and hostile lands of the southwestern United States. On broiling days crusts of salt form on the birds' bills. All animals have to keep a balance between the amount of salt and the amount of water in their bodies. By excreting some salt through its nostrils, the roadrunner reduces its need for water.

But winter nights are cold. When the sun rises the bird lifts its feathers, exposing black skin on its neck and back to the warming rays. This dark skin soaks in the heat of the sun more efficiently than the light sands of the desert. Recharged, the roadrunner is ready to hunt in the still-chilly air.

The bird stalks warily up to a clump of grass and then suddenly rushes, with wings and tail spread wide. A grass-

A roadrunner, with its feathers fluffed, warming itself in the morning sunlight.

hopper, frightened, leaps away. In pursuit, the roadrunner bounds three feet into the air and crushes the insect with one snap of its strong bill.

The search continues for bird eggs, centipedes, scorpions, tarantulas, horned toads, mice, small rats—even fruits and seeds.

A racing roadrunner hears some little squeals. Perhaps a baby bird is in trouble—easy prey. Raising a wing helps the hunter steer quickly toward the sound.

Then a lizard crosses the roadrunner's path. The squeaks are forgotten as the big bird pounces. It catches the lizard by the tail—but that is all it gets. The roadrunner watches the rest of the reptile scramble away unhurt. In time it will grow a new tail.

Darting about, the bird soon finds another lizard. It quickly snaps its beak around the neck—no more tricks. The lizard twists in the strong pincers. The roadrunner slams it against the baked earth until it is limp. Then the bird raises its head and juggles the victim in its mouth until it can be swallowed, head first, in a gulp or two. Lizard gone, the roadrunner is off again on the hunt.

It finds a welcome water hole in the arid land. After a hasty drink, the busy bird settles down, for once, to wait. As the day grows warmer, insects begin to fly. Swifts follow them. First one and then another of the birds swoop down to sip the water while still on the wing. The roadrunner jumps up and snares a swift. Hunting is good.

If you watch a roadrunner race and chase, lurk and leap, you feel it must be always hungry. When the same bird has a nestful of insatiable youngsters waiting for food, it has to multiply its success as a hunter many times.

Roadsides are sure places to find something to eat— the remains of snakes, lizards, and tortoises mown down by motorists. Roadrunners realize this, but they were named long before highways became the butcher shops of the desert. They paced the wagons that first lurched across the sands. Then early automobiles appeared, even more challenging to race. Roadrunners still try to keep up with modern cars at times, but their interest is brief. With a top speed of twenty miles an hour, the birds are soon left behind in the dust.

Other names for the roadrunner are "Snake Bird" and "Ground Cuckoo." The second is as apt as the first, since the roadrunner belongs to the cuckoo family. Its worldwide members have many strange ways. In their habits, some resemble unrelated species more closely than their own cuckoo kin.

Why are such varied birds grouped into a single family? The roadrunner gives some answers. It is streaked with brown and buff, and most other cuckoos are also dressed in neutral colors.

On the roadrunner's cheek is a featherless line which shades from blue to orange. Other members of the cuckoo family also have bare, bright patches of skin emphasizing their eyes.

Most birds have three toes pointing forward and one, the first or "big" toe, in the rear. But cuckoos are zygodactyl, with both their first and fourth toes aiming backwards. Although such feet are best adapted to perching, they do not slow the roadrunner down.

Loose feathers, strong bills, and lengthy tails are characteristic of cuckoos. The roadrunner outdoes many of them with a tail longer than its body, a handy one that acts as a balancing pole.

This family of birds was named for the call of the

male European Cuckoo. Because the cry is given over and over again, with no variation, people used "cuckoo" to describe something as dull and repetitious—then foolish— or even crazy. But the different ways the birds have adapted to life in wilderness and farmland, desert and rain forest, prove that they are far from mad. And the habits they have developed are fascinating.

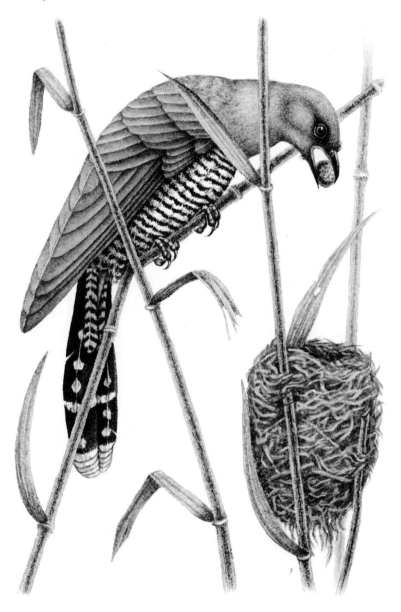

European Cuckoo

Cuckoo-clock Cuckoos

COMMON CUCKOOS

The cry of the male European or Common Cuckoo has been made famous by the clocks that imitate it. Every hour, or sometimes every fifteen minutes, a little door in the clock snaps open and a tiny wooden bird pops out, to the sound of "Cuckoo."

These birds are also known for their odd habits as parents. They do not raise their own young. Instead, their eggs are laid in the nests of other species. These host birds, without seeming to realize it, play foster parents to the baby cuckoos. Because they take advantage of other creatures, but give nothing in return, Common Cuckoos are called parasites.

When the female returns to England from Africa in the spring, she flies to the area where she was raised. There she establishes her territory. Most birds defend their

13

territories fiercely against others of their own species. They want to save the best nesting spots and food for their families. They do not chase away other kinds of birds, though, since these choose different places for their nests and have different diets.

The Common Cuckoo is more relaxed. A second female is welcome as long as the birds she selects to raise her young are not the same species favored by the first cuckoo. Then there is no competition in the search for hospitable nests.

The territory of a male overlaps the home areas of several females. He also does not protect it with vigor. Territorial defense normally insures the survival of the new generation of birds, but male cuckoos are even less involved in the future of their families than the females.

The cuckoos are as unfaithful partners as they are parents. The female's bubbling call can attract a number of males, and she may mate with several of them. And a male does not limit his attentions to a single female.

The future mother must find foster homes for her eggs. Each cuckoo uses the nests of a single species of bird —probably the one that raised her. Although the Common Cuckoos lay eggs with a variety of patterns and colors, those of any one bird are always the same. They tend to resemble the eggs of the foster species she chooses.

In size and silhouette, flight and coloring, the cuckoo looks somewhat like a European sparrow hawk. When it flies over an area, small birds fear that a predator is near.

Their alarm cries give away the location of their nests. Once she has found a number of nests, the female cuckoo patrols them regularly, seeing how they are taking shape and, later, how many eggs are in them. The sight of a nest stimulates the cuckoo to produce an egg. Four or five days later, she is prepared to lay.

Some birds seem hypnotized by the large, observant visitor nearby, but others attack and chase the cuckoo. She does not fight back. It would be harmful, in her scheme of things, to injure the future parents of her young. But she is persistent and returns to the same nests over and over again until she successfully lays her eggs in them.

As the cuckoo watches the nests, she makes sure that they will be ready when she is. Some birds begin incubating with their first eggs, but the small kinds parasitized by cuckoos do not brood before they have completed their "clutches"—the number of eggs typical for their species. Since the embryos only start to develop when warmed by the parents' bodies, the first eggs remain "fresh" until the last is laid. Then the parents take turns on the nest. All the hatchlings break out of their shells at close to the same time, each one equal in size to its sisters and brothers.

If a female cuckoo not ready to lay sees a finished clutch, she may destroy one egg, or all of them. Then the host mother either has to start over again, or at least add another egg to her nest. This gives the cuckoo time to mature one of her own.

The little birds parasitised by cuckoos usually lay in the mornings. Before they have to settle down and incubate, they are free to leave their nests in the afternoons and look for food. The cuckoo lays in the afternoon. She scoots to an unattended nest, deposits an egg in five seconds or less, and then leaves promptly with one of the host's in her bill. She may abandon this—or eat it.

The habit of taking a single egg rather than a nestful seems to increase the success of the cuckoo's parasitism. This was shown by one of the earliest experiments in bird behavior. In 1778 a scientist removed all the eggs from seventeen nests. He replaced each clutch with just one egg of a different species, representing a cuckoo's contribution. All seventeen pairs of birds realized that the solitary eggs meant something was wrong. They deserted their nests.

Since the cuckoo neither incubates nor feeds offspring, she has ample energy to spend on production alone. She lays an egg every other day until she has spotted the landscape with as many as twenty-six. The cuckoo does not immediately ignore the fate of her future children. If the foster parents abandon a nest containing one of her eggs, she will sometimes move it to another site.

The shells of cuckoo eggs are twenty-five percent tougher than those of their hosts. This protects them during their hurried arrival in the world and transportation in the mother's bill. It also helps if the foster parents want to get rid of the strange egg, since they usually start by trying to peck a hole in it.

The cuckoo embryo develops with surprising speed. Its growth begins while the egg is still in the mother's body. With this head start, the cuckoo hatches after twelve and a half days, while the host chicks do not appear for thirteen to fourteen.

The cuckoo's many eggs, their strong shells, and the embryo's speedy growth are needed if the birds are to survive as a species despite their risky reproduction methods. Even so, about forty percent of the young die before leaving the nest. In one study, although sixty-two out of a hundred cuckoo eggs hatched successfully, only twenty-seven of the babies were still alive after twenty days.

When the cuckoo chick is about ten hours old, it develops abnormally sensitive skin in a hollow area of its back, between its rudimentary wings. Anything touching this spot causes the hatchling great discomfort. Instinct demands that the blind and naked little creature struggle and wriggle and push until it can reach the edge of the nest and roll the disturbing object away.

Although the baby will treat an acorn this way, the distressing things it works so hard to eject are usually the eggs and young of its host. Four days later, pinfeathers start to appear on the chick's back, and the skin loses its sensitivity. By then the baby cuckoo is alone in the nest.

This inborn violence of a tiny, undeveloped creature

may seem appalling, but it is the only way the chick can live. The foster parents, no matter how busily they search for insects, can provide only so much food. The cuckoo needs it all. It weighs about one-fourteenth of an ounce at hatching. That increases, by fifty times, to over three-and-a-half ounces when it is ready to leave the nest. Often the whole natural brood of the hosts would not weigh more than the single cuckoo. It cannot afford to be generous and share the nourishment.

Although some birds abandon cuckoo eggs, once the babies hatch they are adopted with enthusiasm by their foster parents. Adults have an instinctive reaction to the wide, begging beaks of young birds. Whether the bill belongs to one of their own or not, it must be stuffed with food.

The open mouth of a cuckoo chick, called its "gape," is orange with yellow edges. Big and bright, it almost shouts, "Feed me!" The foster parents respond, driving themselves close to exhaustion as they try to fill the bottomless stomach.

The reaction of the hosts to a gape is automatic. Equally automatic are the rules which make the cuckoo's appeal the one they answer, even though their own young, thrown from the nest, may still be clinging to life nearby. These chicks are too feeble to gape. More important, they are in the wrong place. To an adult bird, programmed in a certain way of life, hatchlings are only found snuggled deep in a nest.

Sometimes an ambitious, but weak, infant cuckoo cannot shove a foster brother further than the edge of the nest. Then one of the grown birds finishes the job, pushing the chick over. The adult does not recognize it as a living baby, since it is not where such babies should be. So the parent removes it, as it removes other debris that must be taken care of by a good nestkeeper.

A Reed Warbler feeding its mammoth cuckoo chick a caterpillar.

19

After three weeks the baby cuckoo is a ridiculous sight. It is larger than its adult hosts and much too big for the nest. Its tail hangs over one rim while its bulging breast presses against the opposite side. Sometimes the parents have to stand on its back to reach its always-open mouth. Their heads seem to disappear into this cavern, a sight which inspired Shakespeare to write, in *King Lear*, "The hedge-sparrow fed the cuckoo so long, that it had it[s] head bit off by [the] young."

When the baby leaves the nest, it is in danger. So are its hosts. The large, conspicuous cuckoo is much more likely to attract the attention of predators than the small, discreet offspring of the foster parents. Still, they feed this odd and outsized chick for another two or three weeks. The lure of its brilliant gape is so strong that even birds other than cuckoos and their hosts sometimes stop by to drop a morsel into the yawning beak.

Since cuckoos eat insects, they usually parasitise species with similar tastes. Occasionally seed-eating linnets or bullfinchs are used, but these birds, despite their adult diet, bring their young more easily digested bugs. If, by accident, a cuckoo hatches in the nest of complete vegetarians, it will be undernourished.

Whatever the cuckoo is fed at first, once it is on its own, it will favor caterpillars. This is an instinctive taste, not one the bird has to learn. Cuckoos like many hairy and horned insects that are shunned by other species.

As the days become cooler, and the caterpillars wrap

themselves in cocoons, it is time for the young cuckoos to fly south for the winter, like the parents they never knew.

When spring comes again, the females return to their breeding grounds. Each watches for nests of the one kind of bird to which she entrusts her eggs.

The males are also back, and alert for available mates. Their cuckoo calls sound through the woods, ringing notes that can be heard a mile away.

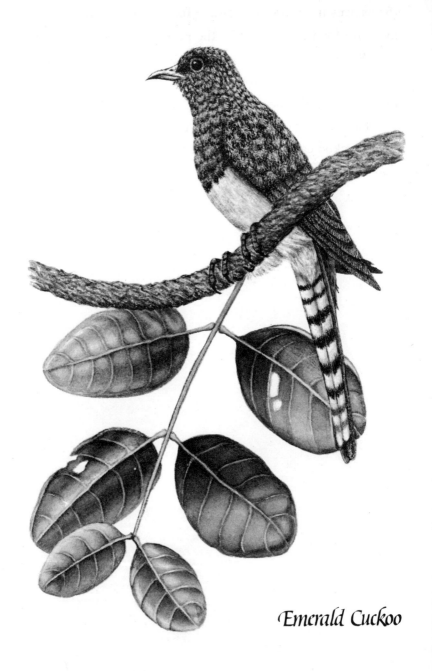

Emerald Cuckoo

Puzzling Parents

PARASITISM

Cuckoos probably first developed on earth some thirty-six to forty million years ago. The earliest fossil, *Dynamopterus*, was found in France. Now some one hundred and thirty different species of the family live all around the globe.

Aptly, the most widespread is the Common Cuckoo. It breeds throughout much of the Old World of Europe, Africa and Asia and lays its eggs in the nests of close to three hundred kinds of birds. It belongs to a subfamily of the cuckoos containing thirty-one species, all parasites, living in the Old World.

The large cuckoo family has five other subfamilies. One includes three species in South America, part of the New World, that rely on strange birds to care for their offspring. All the others raise their own children, but the bad reputation of the minority, the parasites, is often associated with cuckoos in general.

There are different types of parasites. Among them are the ticks that suck blood from dogs wandering through bushy country, or from human hikers. These are ectoparasites, like leeches, that attack the skin of their victims. Endoparasites, such as tapeworms, live inside their hosts' bodies.

Cuckoos, of course, are neither endo- nor ectoparasites. The survival of their young depends on the behavior of the hosts in relation to their families, or broods. So the cuckoos that lay in the nests of others are called "brood parasites."

All brood parasites do not have the same habits. Some leave more than one egg in a nest. Since most hatchlings do not have the sensitive skin which demands the removal of other objects, many kinds of cuckoos grow up with their step-chicks. However, if its nestmates are smaller, the noisy demands and brilliant gape of a baby cuckoo can keep the adults too busy to worry about their own children. They starve to death.

Certain unusually colorful cuckoos in Africa have not completely given up tending their offspring. The Didrics, dressed in bright shades with metallic sheens, aid the foster parents in feeding the young cuckoos once they have left the nest. Other cuckoos have never been seen to do this, not even the closely related Emerald Cuckoo, the most brilliant one of all. Some scientists think this behavior might represent a middle stage in the development of parasitic habits—somewhere between a bird's raising its own brood and another's laying eggs as her only contribution to the continuation of the species.

Although their means of insuring that their chicks survive may differ, many cuckoos have become brood parasites. Even more have not. Why? This is a question with no final answer so far. But scientific studies have arrived at some suggestions.

Many brood parasites do not choose a single mate. The males, particularly, are promiscuous. Without a close tie to one female, a male may lose interest in protecting the territory where she is tending the family he fathered.

The loss of the urge to defend a home range might lead to the loss of the nest-building instinct itself. However, it may be a case of which came first, like the riddle of the chicken and the egg. Did a weakening of the compulsion to build nests lead to casual relationships with several partners and, finally, the males' disinterest in defending territories—or was it the other way around?

Many birds use old nests of other species, or even drive a nest-maker away from its own construction. Starlings take over woodpeckers' holes this way. That might be one of the first steps in developing a habit of putting eggs in strange places.

Another possibility is that the mother was not near her own home when it was time to lay. She might have been far afield hunting food, or something might have destroyed her nest before she could use it. Perhaps the internal clock which times the birds' reproductive activities —mating, building, laying, incubating, feeding—broke down, telling the female to start producing before it told her to collect twigs. The drive to complete the steps of family life is very strong. Gulls with an urge to brood will try to incubate golf balls and tin cans.

This built-in clock is powered to a great degree by hormones. Different amounts in a bird's blood at different times stimulate the right behavior at each stage of the reproductive cycle. A study of cowbirds, also brood parasites, suggests that such birds do not lack hormones. They had as high a level of one as did Red-winged Blackbirds, who bring up their own families in more normal ways. However, the cowbirds' reaction to the chemical stimuli was obviously not the same. Perhaps brood parasites have nervous systems that are insensitive, for some reason, to the hormones.

Other studies of cowbirds hint at the further development of brood parasitism. Although a Bay-winged Cowbird may build a nest now and then, it usually takes over another bird's. A second Bay-wing may not even make the effort to find a nest she can usurp. She lays her eggs in the one claimed by the first female, who cares for the whole brood. She has successfully parasitised a member of her own species.

The next step in the growing habit is shown by the Screaming Cowbird. It does not use its fellows as foster parents, but its close kin, the put-upon Bay-winged.

When some birds were first experimenting with brood parasitism, they probably had to use relatives as hosts, as the Screaming Cowbird does. Because eggs of the two species would look much alike, one laid by an imposter is accepted easily. But if a single type of foster parent is used, it could become overexploited. The survival of the host would be in doubt, and this, in turn, would threaten the survival of the brood parasite.

So a parasitic species benefits if its eggs are accepted by a large number of species. But such a variety of hosts would also have eggs of many sizes, colors and patterns.

Birds react in different ways to unusual eggs in their nests. They may ignore them, as the Hedge Sparrow does: this tolerant creature will even try to incubate pebbles. Some start building all over again, making their new nests right on top of the old ones—and the unwanted cuckoo eggs. Still others desert an invaded nest and begin another somewhere else.

A fourth reaction is to get rid of the bothersome cuckoo egg, if possible. Many birds throw strange objects out of their nests. This does not mean that they know what their own eggs look like. They just recognize that something is amiss. Once three eggs from the incomplete clutch of a warbler were removed and three of a sparrow substituted. Then the warbler laid a fourth egg. Since it did not match the others in the nest, she threw it overboard.

To insure success as brood parasites, therefore, it

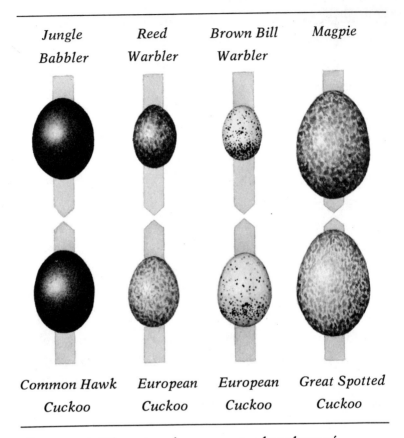

The eggs of different cuckoos compared to those of
the species they parasitize.

would help a species if its eggs closely matched those of
as many hosts as possible. In England, although cuckoo
eggs are occasionally found in the nests of fifty different
species, only about six are parasitised regularly. These are
all little birds, like wrens and sparrows. So the cuckoo's
eggs have also become smaller than would be expected of

animals their size—only $\frac{1}{33}$ the weight of the mother. The Great Spotted Cuckoo, though, lays in the nests of husky crows and magpies. Its eggs are larger than normal, equal to $\frac{1}{11}$ of the female cuckoo's weight.

The need to imitate the hosts' eggs has led to a great variety of patterns and colors in the cuckoos'. They became blue, tan, white—spotted, streaked or splotched—as each female's production developed closer and closer to that of the bird she used. In Finland, sixty-eight percent of the cuckoos' eggs are blue, like those of its main hosts—whinchats, wheatears, redstarts and flycatchers. In Hungary the eggs tend more to green, patched with brown, matching the eggs of the most important foster species, the Great Reed Warbler.

How closely the eggs of the cuckoos copy those of their hosts varies. In southern England, where the birds parasitise quite a few other species, their eggs have a generalized color which blends into the contents of a number of nests without exactly imitating them.

The mimicry of the cuckoos in Asia is more advanced. This suggests that parasitism started earlier in the East and had time to develop further. Even an ornithologist, a scientist specializing in birds, cannot tell the difference between the eggs of the hosts and those of the Great Spotted and Hawk Cuckoos. The latter, as its name suggests, also resembles predators feared by the species they parasitise. Their repeated calls have earned them the title "Brainfever Birds" in India, where the incessant sound is supposed to drive the listeners mad.

In Australia, another cuckoo, the koel, parasitises a variety of victims, from carnivorous shrikes to beautiful birds of paradise. The eggs differ accordingly.

However, the koels of India only lay in the nests of House Crows. Their eggs copy the crows' quite closely, but their mimicry goes further than that. Although the adult males are black, and the females brown with light spots, youngsters of both sexes are totally black, like the baby crows.

Some cuckoos resemble the adults of the birds they parasitise. The Drongo Cuckoo of Asia relies on the black, swallow-tailed Drongos to take care of its chicks. It also has black plumage and a swallow-tail, the only tail of that sort in the whole diverse cuckoo family.

In all these ways, the parasitic cuckoos have developed characteristics which make either them, their young or their eggs acceptable to the birds whose help they need. Natural selection has intensified these traits. Foster parents are more likely to incubate an egg much like their own and to raise its infant occupant successfully. When that chick grows up, its eggs will continue to be a close match to those of the host species.

The egg that is a poor imitation will be refused. The embryo inside dies without a chance to duplicate, in its own eggs, the wrong patterns and colors. So, generation after generation, the cuckoos' mimicry grows nearer and nearer to its models.

Among the Asian members of the parasitic subfamily is the Shining Cuckoo. While roadrunners and many other cuckoos are content to stay at home, this species makes an outstanding migratory flight. The female lays in the nests of non-migratory birds on the islands off New Zealand. Once that is done, the adults leave.

A month later the young cuckoos desert their foster parents and head west toward Australia. Then, without an older guide or earlier experience of the way, they turn north to continue their journey. After winging more than two thousand miles across the uncharted Pacific, the young Shining Cuckoos arrive at the Bismarck and Solomon Islands. The parents are already there.

Yellow-billed Cuckoo

Cow-cows &
Chow-chows

NORTH AMERICAN CUCKOOS

While instinct is guiding the Shining Cuckoos on their fall migration below the equator, it is spring in the Northern Hemisphere. Yellow-billed and Black-billed Cuckoos are arriving in their breeding grounds across the United States and into southern Canada.

These birds are slim and trim, slightly larger than robins. Perfectly streamlined, they fly with speed and grace, unlike the shaggy roadrunners. Both species are neatly clad in dull brown feathers above and paler plumage below. They have long, black tails with white spots on the underside, small ones for the Black-bill and larger ones for the Yellow-bill. The latter can also be identified by its rusty wings and yellow lower beak.

The cuckoos are shy birds. They slip through the woods, hiding beneath sun-spotted foliage. The light from above, even filtered through leaves, is strong enough to brighten their dark backs. Shadows from the woodland floor dim the cuckoos' whitish breasts. Counter-shaded, they become ghosts, melting into the sun and shade patterns of the forest background.

The furtive, counter-shaded cuckoos might escape from notice except for their calls—long strings of "ki-ki-ki-ki-kowp-kowp-kowp-kowup" for the Yellow-bill and a hurried "kukuku-kukuku-kukukuku-kukuku" or repeated "kuks" for the Black-bill. People have translated these sounds into popular names, "Cow-cow" and "Chow-chow."

When the sky is heavy with threatening clouds, the woods are hushed, waiting for the storm to break. This is one time the cuckoos call frequently. They can easily be heard in the silence. Humans listened and gave them other names, "Storm Crow," "Rain Crow," and "Rain Dove." Since downpours did follow the cries, some people believed that the birds actually brought the rain. Of course, even Storm Crows have no such power. If only they had, farmers in drought-stricken areas would coax them to sing day and night.

The Black-bill does often call at night, when its rapid, rhythmic notes break the stillness. It is also more apt to feed on the ground and visit streams or ponds than the Yellow-bill. There it adds water bugs and small aquatic animals to its diet.

Both of the North American cuckoos build their own nests, four to ten feet high, in trees and shrubs. These secretive birds prefer bushes hidden by viney curtains. The nests are casual collections of sticks, roots and such, with thin linings of softer grass, pine needles or catkins. They are flat and frail affairs. Someone on the ground can often count the number of eggs by looking right up through the flimsy constructions. Eggs occasionally roll out of the rickety shelters, or are brushed off by the parents.

The birds lay two to five bluish-green eggs. They start incubation before the clutch is complete, resulting in nests that may contain a fresh egg, a developing one, and chicks of various ages.

After about two weeks of incubation, an infant cuckoo hatches. From the very first, it is remarkably strong. At the old age of three hours, one could hang from a twig by its foot, or even a single toe, for fifteen seconds. Soon a baby can pull itself up onto a branch by its scrawny but sturdy legs, quite an acrobatic feat for a tiny hatchling not long out of its shell.

Like all nestlings, small cuckoos lie flat against the bottom of their home with their feet wrapped tightly around some part of it. Remove a baby and it will tear the nest before releasing its hold. This is an instinct as strong as the one that tells an infant ape to clutch its mother's fur. Outside the nest, an unhappy chick will open and close its toes in a reflex action that only stops at the touch of something firm it can grab.

The little cuckoos never grow a soft coat of baby down. Instead they become odd-looking birds, with a

*A Black-billed Cuckoo on its nest. The narrow bands
of white on the tips of its tail feathers distinguish
it from the Yellow-bill.*

certain resemblance to porcupines. Their skin is black,
tough, and leathery. As each real feather comes through, it
is covered with a pointed sheath. The babies seem to be
wearing an armor of dark quills.

The courage of these ugly youngsters matches their
strength. If alarmed, they raise the sharp sheaths, vibrate
their miniature wings, and buzz like a hive of bees. Before
they can fly, they will escape an intruder by leaving the
nest. They climb into the shelter of shrubbery by crooking
their necks and wings and clinging with their feet.

One scientist caught a seven-day-old Yellow-billed

chick. He placed it on the ground near his camera. He wanted to record the opening of the feather sheaths. At ten thirty in the morning they began to split. The man compared the process to the commotion in a corn popper, or a flower's bursting into bloom.

The cuckoo's sheaths broke to reveal fully formed feathers. By three in the afternoon, the little chick was almost clothed in proper cuckoo plumage, lacking only the adult's long tail.

Another scientist watched a Black-billed Cuckoo while this phenomenon occurred. He tells a slightly different story. On the sixth day of its life, the bird began to run its bill over the feather covers, starting at the bottom of each. By the end of the next day, the bases of the sheaths were detached, and the nestling pulled them off by the beakful.

While still half-quilled, half-feathered, the chick left its nest. It jumped out and caught a twig in its feet. After dangling topsy turvy for a moment, it pulled itself up and settled down on the branch.

Most young cuckoos leave home when they are seven to nine days old. Unable to fly for another two weeks, they spend the time climbing in the greenery near the nests and waiting for the adults to bring them food.

Both parents take their duties seriously. They tend the eggs, feed the babies, and risk their own lives by trying to lure enemies away from the helpless young. However, the females do occasionally drop eggs in the nests of other birds. Usually a Yellow-billed Cuckoo donates an egg to a

Black-billed, or the other way around, but sometimes the host is of unrelated species, such as catbirds, cardinals or thrushes. Perhaps the mother does this because, when she is ready to lay, her own sloppy nest has fallen apart.

A large and growing young cuckoo was seen to push two Golden Warbler babies out of the nest they shared. Even though the observer returned the ousted infants as close to the nest as possible, the parents ignored them. They concentrated on the demands of the biggest chick.

This nestling was well able to take care of itself, but one of the adult cuckoos did not seem sure. Restlessly flitting from branch to branch, she haunted the area where her baby was being tended by others. Unlike the Common Cuckoos, she still retained some mothering instinct.

Another cuckoo laid two eggs in a robin's nest. The robin added one of her own. Then a Mourning Dove, another unskilled nest builder, contributed two more to the assortment. Later the cuckoo and the dove were seen seated side by side on the nest, brooding together. Sadly, there is no last chapter to this story. The man who found the mixed family in 1827 took the eggs and nest to study.

Young cuckoos would thrive under a robin's care on nourishing worms. But the dove's diet of seeds and fruit would have left the babies famished.

While the North American cuckoos enjoy a taste of wild grapes or berries in season, they are, like their Common cousins, insectivorous. They eat grasshoppers, spiders, flies, ants, beetles, wasps, and, most welcome of all, caterpillars. Their hearty appetite for spiked and hairy ones makes them firm allies of farmers and gardeners. Several cuckoos have been found to have over one hundred tent caterpillars in their stomachs.

Eventually a cuckoo's stomach becomes padded with thick felt and it has difficulty digesting its food. Other birds lose the linings of their stomachs slowly and continually, just as humans constantly replace their skin cells. But the cuckoos actually shed theirs all at once, along with the matted hair and spines. With new linings already growing, they are soon ready to clear out trees hung with caterpillar tents or fields attacked by locusts once more.

The cuckoos arrive rather late in the spring. Those that migrate as far north as New England may not build their nests until June. But, if the insect crops are poor, they start back to Columbia, Peru, and Uruguay as early as the end of July.

The cuckoos will stay long after their parental duties are over, though, if they find a vigorous webworm infestation or other source of abundant food. They follow their prey and become unusually common in areas crowded with insects. It is thought that they will even lay more eggs if their nests are in the midst of woods or fields particularly plagued with bugs.

Finally the summer ends and the insects die or disappear. By the last of September, any lingering cuckoos escape the coming cold and head for the warmth of the South American tropics for the winter.

Smooth-billed Ani

Groove-billed Ani

Amiable Anis

COMMUNAL CUCKOOS

Roadrunners and the North American Black- and Yellow-bills sometimes place their eggs haphazardly. The Common Cuckoos and their kin are parasites. Another subfamily, living in the New World, has developed a still different approach to parenthood—group nests. Among its members are the anis.

These birds have almost bare, black faces and plumage dark as tar. They look sloppily put together, with short, loose-jointed wings and long, ragged tails. Flying or walking, the birds are clownishly awkward. When one glides to the ground, it runs a few paces, stops—and then may topple as its tail sails on with a momentum of its own.

The upper bills of the anis are narrow and highly arched, giving them profiles like parrots. The top beak of the Smooth-bill is unmarked, while three indented lines run the length of the Groove-bill's.

Both species live in flocks that roost together at night. Although they prefer open, grassy country for finding food, it must be dotted with trees and bushes where they can rest and nest.

In the morning a colony leaves its roost to hunt for insects. The birds scatter across the savanna, but stay within calling distance of each other. They often follow cattle to catch bugs flushed from the grass by the grazing beasts. With great excitement, they also pursue insects stirred up by advancing columns of army ants.

The anis dislike cold and rain. If they have to forage in wet grass, they fly up to a sunny branch as soon as they can and spread their wings to dry. The row of pitch black birds resembles a gathering of miniature vultures.

Some Smooth-billed Anis live permanently in Florida, and Groove-billed ones in Texas. In addition, wanderers of both species are seen occasionally in the far south of the United States, but their main range is from Central America to northern South America. Although they do not migrate, they are still dependent on the seasons.

From November to the middle of May, the weather is dry. Since insects are scarce, the Smooth-billed Anis live on palm fruits, berries and seeds. When the rains come, they return to a diet of insects, small lizards, and perhaps baby birds of other species. Possibly this change to animal food stimulates the urge to mate. The wet season is their breeding time.

The Smooth-billed males court the females by whining, twitching their tails up and down, and carrying gifts of leaves in their bills. In some colonies each bird has just one mate, while in others they appear to be polygamous.

Whether the males are fickle or faithful, they join the females in building coarse nests, one foot across, of twigs and little branches. Then, up to five anis lay their eggs together, four to seven apiece. The final clutch in the crowded nest may reach a total of thirty.

This is not an efficient way to raise baby birds. Some eggs fall out. Others are woven into the nest by anis that continue to build while their comrades are laying. And the sheer mass of the eggs keeps them from being incubated evenly.

Once there were four eggs on the ground below a nest. Although they had fallen five days before, one contained a tiny embryo whose heart was still beating, despite its long abandonment. This toughness of their babies does not turn the anis into successful parents, though. Only a third of the nine eggs left in the nest hatched—and then all three chicks disappeared.

A very small flock of one male and two female Smooth-bills built six nests in less than four months. They produced at least thirty-four eggs. All of them were lost. An observer, unable to watch the nests every moment, never

43

learned what caused this depressing mortality rate. It might have been due to poor housekeeping or to raids by reptiles, small mammals and predatory birds. Or it might have been some combination of these problems.

If and when the Smooth-billed chicks hatch, they are cared for by much of the flock, although just one male always guards the nest at night. One brood, the offspring of two females, was fed·by nine of the fifteen colony members. The little anis make a sizzling noise, like bacon frying, when they are hungry—most of the time. They will try to eat anything, from a stick jutting above the nest rim to the fingertip of a curious scientist.

When one adult bird brings an insect too large for the young, it waits for the arrival of another. The two play tug-of-war with the oversized mouthful until it is torn into baby food.

The communal nests are located in a territory of about ten acres. All the Smooth-bills defend the area hotly if a strange ani tries to encroach. The intruder may be chased repeatedly by one angry resident, or the whole flock may rush the bird to speed its departure.

When several Smooth-billed Anis belonging to different colonies were captured and put in a cage far from their territories, though, there was no hostility. Outside their home grounds, their natural sociability asserted itself. They roosted in a row, side by side, from the very first night.

The Groove-billed Anis are even more amiable than

44

their Smooth-billed cousins. They make little attempt to claim a range of their own. The territorial defense of most birds is thought to keep their numbers from growing larger than local food supplies can support. This same result, population control, is reached by the inefficient nesting habits of the anis.

When the rainy season starts, the Groove-bills pair off, although the couples stay with the flock. They are monogamous and apparently very affectionate. A scientist described one couple as acting like newlyweds. They perched together as closely as they could and preened each other at length. When the eggs were laid, the bird incubating and its nearby mate called to each other constantly. Sometimes the one on the nest played hookey briefly for a quick cuddle with the other.

As time passed, the birds became more like old married folks, absorbed by their family obligations. The man watching the two decided that their parental instincts had not been weakened. The anis took good care of their young and defended them staunchly. Their communal nests seemed to be the result of intense sociability, not a step along the road to brood parasitism.

Half of the nests studied belonged to single pairs, while the others were built by up to three couples, rarely more. Each female laid from three to five eggs, and the largest clutch found contained fifteen. How many nests are made by groups and how many by two birds may depend on the number of good sites available. The anis prefer to

Ani chick about six days old wearing feather sheaths.
Its tail feathers are beginning to grow out
of the tubes.

build in thorny, densely-leaved orange trees, thick tangles of vines or other secret spots. If choice places are limited, the friendly birds share.

Usually the male ferries sticks and straw and other rough materials to the female, who does the actual construction. The nest is lined with green leaves. When the adults are incubating and the time comes for one bird to replace another, it arrives with a fresh leaf in its bill. This way the lining is constantly renewed as long as the nest is used.

Only a portion of the Groove-billed Anis' eggs hatch, but their success is greater than that of the Smooth-billed. Perhaps the smaller number of eggs in the group nests helps, or perhaps the greater dedication of monogamous couples boosts the survival rate.

The newborn young of both species are black, blind and naked. Feather sheaths, like those of the Yellow-billed and Black-billed Cuckoos, appear rapidly. Some time between the fourth and sixth days the ungainly little ones are strong enough to respond to their parents' alarm calls. They scramble out of their nests and hoist themselves by necks, wings and legs into the sheltering leaves, or drop to the ground, where they scuttle for cover under the grass.

When the emergency is over, the chicks return, if they can, to be brooded a little longer. On the ninth day, the Groove-billed young leave their nests, but they spend the next two days in the tree where they hatched. Then, feathered and fearless, they practice short flights in the brush before their parents lead them out to forage with the flock.

The Groove-billed Anis are preoccupied with family throughout the rainy season and may have two broods or more. Infants have been seen late in September, not long before the dry days begin in November.

The earlier young stay with their flocks and even with their families. One Groove-bill, two-and-a-half months old, defended the nest in its parents' absence and helped feed the new hatchlings. As sociable as its elders, it nibbled their feathers companionably. When one of the adults brooded the babies, the older offspring sometimes kept it company, sitting on the edge of the nest.

The young of the Smooth-billed Anis also join the rest of the colony in finding insects for their new siblings. They stay with the group for many months, but probably leave before the rains return, bringing the start of another breeding season. Only about thirty-five percent of the hatchlings reach this stage.

Despite the rather dismal survival rate of their eggs and infants, the anis are good parents when they have the chance. They also have other talents which help the two species thrive.

The Smooth-billed Anis show a remarkable ability to learn what is best to do in new situations. The sight of a human usually makes them flee in fear. But, if a farmer is working with a scythe or hoe, frightened bugs spring from cover around him. The eager anis then approach within a few feet to reap the harvest. They have also discovered that mowing machines, though noisier than cattle, are just as harmless—and efficient in arousing insects.

The Smooth-billed Anis make the most of their savanna homes, but the Groove-billed are more adaptable, a useful thing for a bird to be. Most creatures are dependent on one kind of habitat. If it is destroyed, so is the species. The plight of the many endangered animals today illustrates this all too well.

48

The Groove-billed Anis, though, can live almost anywhere in their range, except the depths of dense rain forests. But a clearing in these damp woods will attract them. Even a marshland can become home, if there are enough trees and bushes in its soggy expanse. At the other extreme are arid semi-desert regions, where the birds hide their nests in the prickly protection of cacti. The anis take the greatest possible advantage of their environment, wet or dry, in the close company of their fellows.

Hoatzin

What is a "Wattzin"?

THE HOATZIN

"Wattzin" is the way you pronounce "hoatzin," the name of the oddest cuckoo of all. It lives in South America, but has a much more limited range than the anis. The birds stay by great rivers, the Amazon and Orinoco, and their tributaries.

One of the hoatzin's nicknames is "Reptile Bird," since the creatures smell, sound, and even, in some ways, look like reptiles. They are primitive animals that exist mainly on a diet of leaves. The need to digest such coarse fare has led to bodily changes unknown in other birds.

The hoatzin is so unusual that its exact place in the world of ornithology puzzled scientists for years. Until recently it was put in its own family, part of the order of fowls, such as partridges and turkeys. "Hoatzin" comes from a Brazilian Indian word which Europeans misinterpreted as "pheasant." Other cuckoos have also been named after pheasants and peacocks.

As long ago as 1829, some scientists found features they felt were closer to cuckoos than fowls. Studies of feathers, arteries, bones, muscles and behavior kept hinting, through the years, at some relationship between the hoatzin and the cuckoo family.

Techniques for classifying birds are becoming more and more sophisticated—and harder for untrained people to understand than similarities between beaks and bones. Chemical and electrical experiments reveal the secrets of birds today.

Dr. Charles Sibley and Dr. Jon Ahlquist, of Yale University, used such advanced techniques to study egg whites. When proteins in the whites of hoatzin eggs were exposed to electrical fields, their reactions closely matched those of another bird, the guira.

These recent tests put the hoatzin in the same cuckoo subfamily as the guira. The anis are also members of this subfamily, which is divided into three genera, one for each type of bird.

The guira's behavior in many ways resembles that of its South American neighbors and relatives, the anis. It is a communal bird that lives in a territory of rich savanna only slackly defended by the colony. There, bulky, leaf-lined nests are made by either one pair or a number of birds. But the Groove-billed Anis' dedication to parenthood seems to be lacking in the guiras. The adults may hustle food to the chicks every ten minutes or visit them less than once each hour. Perhaps these haphazard habits make social nesting important for the birds. Babies would have a better chance if tended by quite a few of such absentminded guardians.

The guiras do not look like their ani relatives. Their coats are not coal black, but brown-streaked above and lighter below.

The hoatzin has the same coloring as the guira, but it is larger and outlandish in appearance. The long, shaggy crest of the hoatzin is comically dishevelled. Its red eyes are surrounded by wrinkled blue skin, and its feathers might have been glued in place, one at a time, by a little child in a very great hurry.

Hoatzins eat small fish and crabs from time to time, or tender flowers, but their main food is the tough fruit and leaves of riverside plants, such as mangrove and mukkamukka. Most birds first store what they eat in their crops, an area of the digestive tract between the mouth and the stomach. The food then passes on to the part of the stomach known as the gizzard, where it is ground with the aid of small stones, or grit. The hoatzins have developed huge crops, though, holding fifty times more than their gizzards. There horny, muscular linings help squeeze nourishment from fibrous diet.

After a hoatzin feeds for a long time, its crop becomes so heavy that it has to lean on a branch for support. The birds have calloused pads on their chests to protect them against abrasion. Their breastbones, or sternums, include flat disks that help hold up the weight of leafy feasts.

Their sternums have grown smaller than those of most birds to make room for the great crops, which fill the front third of the hoatzins' bodies. Since breastbones anchor the flight muscles, these shallow ones limit the birds' flying ability. They flounder through trees and lurch across narrow streams, ending their efforts in clumsy crash landings. Perhaps the hoatzins are sedentary because they are so awkward in the air. Year after year they can be found in the same areas, often in the same trees.

Hoatzins clamber through the foliage in flocks of ten to thirty. When the rains come, they split into breeding groups of two to six. They seem to mate rather casually and are probably promiscuous. The members of each small band cooperate in building one nest, a rough construction of sticks in the fork of a tree branch.

The tan eggs, spotted with blue, brown, or pink, are cared for by all the adults. Incubation starts after the first is laid and takes a full four weeks. Then the hatchlings appear, one after another. Their eyes are already open, unlike those of other cuckoo chicks, and they wear a thin coat of down, the first of two. The infants also have two claws on the front edge of each wing. The claws are on the

54

tips of what once were the index fingers and thumbs of ancient reptiles, the ancestors of birds.

Fossils about 140 million years old show fingertip claws on the wings of a creature that was named *Archae-opteryx*, or "ancient wing." Some scientists consider this feathered animal an early bird, while others classify it as one of the last, warmblooded reptiles on the evolutionary path that led to birds.

The hoatzins' primitive claws are handy for the hatch-

An infant hoatzin climbs with the help of its neck, feet,
and four wing claws. After about two weeks,
the claws drop off, but the baby will still use its neck
and wings while clambering through the branches.

lings. Many young cuckoos scramble through foliage around their nests before they are able to fly. With nails to help, the infant hoatzins are the ablest acrobats of all. The claws drop off as the chicks' grownup feathers appear, just in time. The clumsy creatures could not afford any more obstacles to flight, and claws create more turbulence than sleek, smooth wings. A few other birds have nails they keep throughout their lives. But they are either so tiny that they are hidden by feathers, as in swifts, or they belong to flightless birds such as ostriches.

Before a hoatzin nestling is ready to sample the greens near its home, it is fed a mush of mukkamukka leaves. Its pitiful piping reminds the adults that it is hungry. When an older bird opens its mouth, a greedy chick thrusts its head inside to find the predigested, softened stuff it needs.

All the hoatzins try to defend the young. Once, when a baby was testing its climbing skill in a jungle of twigs, five grown birds spread their wings above it. The plumage parasol hid the little explorer from the eyes of predators —and a curious scientist.

The flock objects noisily to the approach of any intruder. Each member croaks hoarsely, while nervously flicking its tail and flapping its wings. A brooding bird will guard the nest just as long as it dares. One let a man get so close it was able to peck him crossly on the nose before it fled.

If it is deserted, a baby hoatzin takes over its own defense effectively. The nests are always built in trees that hang over a river. There are also clear passages, not blocked by branches, under the crude stick platforms. When a tiny infant feels threatened, it climbs to the rim of the nest and dives straight into the water, six to twenty feet below. With hardly a splash, it disappears, leaving widening circles as the only clues to its passage.

The small adventurer swims ably underwater, pushed by the current. Downstream from every nest a snarly mass of vines cloaks the river bank. When it reaches this haven, the soaked escapee scrambles onto land. Hidden by greenery, it squawks, "Squeeonk, squeeonk!" It has done all it can and is calling for help. The grown hoatzins encourage it back to the nest with gentle, growling sounds.

Early this century a famous explorer, scientist, and author, William Beebe, saw a terrified nestling plunge into a river. Five or six minutes after the little bird vanished underwater, he watched as

> a skinny, crooked, two-fingered mitten of an arm reared upward out of the muddy flood and the nestling, black and glistening, hauled itself out of the water. Thus must the first amphibian have climbed into the thin air.

Actually, the first vertebrate to make the transition from sea to shore was probably a fish. Still, Beebe's comparison of the hoatzin chick to an amphibian was appropriate. Many people who have seen the birds write about them in terms of more primitive animals.

Hoatzins, like the anis and other birds, make a wide variety of sounds. They cluck when courting, meow while feeding, wheeze in surprise, and screech with fear. Beebe described their most characteristic cry, though, as a harsh croak like that of the frog, an amphibian. It has also been said to sound more reptilian than birdlike.

Hoatzins have a distinct odor at times. Beebe found it not unpleasant. It reminded him of the circus—a mixture of sawdust, peanuts and lots of elephants. Others thought the smell was closer to a crocodile's. And the babies, with their scrawny necks and beaked faces, have been described as miniature copies of the age-old giant tortoises.

These reptile birds are also called "Stink Birds" and "Stinking Hannahs." This sounds insulting, but the smelly reputation has protected them from close human neighbors. Since the flesh was supposed to be as foul as the odor, they were not hunted for food. The eggs were eaten, though, and some of the blundering birds are shot just for amusement. Monkeys, opossums, tree snakes, and birds of prey will take the eggs and young, but the only serious threat to the harmless hoatzins is the destruction of their limited river bank range.

The birds are too specialized in their own, odd way of life to adapt to a variety of environments, as the Groove-billed Anis do. Once a farmer bulldozed some trees which were the home of a colony. The birds returned to the up-rooted vegetation and stayed there as it died. When the leaves were gone, they died, too, even though other hoat-zins were thriving in an undisturbed grove a hundred feet away.

Red-faced Malkoha

Worldwide Family

MORE CUCKOOS

In a time when so many animals are in danger, it is a relief to hear of birds that can take care of themselves as well as most cuckoos do. Their ability to adapt to different places and ways of life has led to their success. However, at least one species has become extinct within the last half-century, the Delalande's Coua.

This bird lived in northeastern Madagascar and on a smaller island nearby in the Indian Ocean—until its habitat was destroyed. One was seen in late 1929, but, after that, even generous rewards offered to local hunters failed to bring in any more reports. The wild populations of islands are particularly sensitive to human intrusion. If disturbed, they have no other place to go.

Nine other coua species complete this cuckoo subfamily. All are found only in the Malagasy Republic, the modern name for Madagascar, a large island that separated from the mainland of Africa over sixty million years ago. Isolated ocean islands often develop different and distinct forms of animal life, not influenced by immigrants from other lands. The descendants of the original inhabitants change over the years as they fill empty ecological niches— areas of space or behavior not already used by another species.

Through the years some couas became runners, spending most of their time on the ground in fairly open country. Others are arboreal—climbing, leaping, or flying through the forests. By hunting and nesting at different levels or in different areas, the members of the species avoid competing with each other. This adaptation to several niches increases the couas' chances of survival in Madagascar.

Another large island in the Indian Ocean, Ceylon, is the home of an endangered cuckoo, the Red-faced Malkoha. These birds are extinct on the mainland of India and are rare even on the island. Lumbering in the Ceylonese forests threatens their future, but there is a little hope. Some have been seen recently in cultivated areas. They may have an "ecological elasticity"—an ability to adapt to life in a new habitat—missing in the hoatzins and many other species.

Some cuckoos that are already accustomed to sharing

space with human beings are the coucals, a genus whose twenty-seven species are found in Asia and Africa. The coucals are terrestrial birds with short, round wings, and, like roadrunners, they fly with reluctance and little grace.

In Asia the big, black coucals comb orchards, gardens, and even village greens for prey, as well as wilder areas. One, or sometimes two together, stalk through the grass. By jerking their widespread, chestnut-colored wings, the coucals can paralyze large insects with fright. They also hunt on higher levels, hopping nimbly through the trees in the search for young birds and eggs. These they promptly devour.

The coucals are neither parasites nor communal layers. They incubate their own eggs and raise the chicks. Their nests, differing from those of other cuckoos, are round-topped structures with side entrances. Sometimes a short tunnel leads into the domed interior.

A coucal that seems to be an exceptionally concerned parent is the White-browed of Africa. One was seen flying with a chick held firmly between its thighs, probably fleeing a brush fire. The White-browed young cannot protect themselves from flames, but they have a defense against other dangers. They hiss angrily at intruders—and then vomit a dark and sickening liquid over those who ignore the warning.

Other African birds include the Cinderellas of the drab

cuckoo clan. Two of these species are dressed in yellow and iridescent greens, while the third, the Didric Cuckoo, has a coppery sheen on its back, contrasting with its white underside. These small, brilliant birds flit through the upper stories of the rain forest, feeding on insects and a little fruit.

Since the Didrics are parasites, a female watches other birds closely to keep in touch with their family plans. She will eject an egg from a borrowed nest and replace it with one of her own, which hatches before the other infants emerge. But then the pattern changes. After a chick leaves the nest, its real parents may join the foster ones in feeding it. One possible explanation has been suggested for the Didric males, at least. They offer insects as gifts to their mates. Could they confuse the feathered young with females ready for courting?

Squirrel Cuckoos are other gallant males that bring bugs to the females they woo. These South American birds belong to the same subfamily of cuckoos as the more northerly Black- and Yellow-bills, but some of their behavior echoes that of their neighbors, the anis. They live in open areas and pad their nests with leaves. Brown stains from the withered linings soon darken the white eggs. This coloration probably protects eggs exposed to predators in the shallow nests.

These cuckoos build their rickety homes on interwoven tangles of twigs. One female, though, perched on a

A faithful pair of Squirrel Cuckoos with soft feathers of warm brown above and gray below. These birds are named for their habit of hopping and bounding through the trees.

single branch. Her hardworking mate brought her nesting material—over and over again. She stuffed each piece under her, with more confidence than success. Without support, it fell to the ground. After a week the earth beneath the inappropriate site was littered with twigs and leaves—and an egg, laid in the nonexistent nest. The female might have been a young one learning by experience, and very slowly.

Unlike brood parasites and communal nesters, the Squirrel Cuckoos seem to make devoted couples. They are seen in pairs at all seasons of the year. Both parents feed the young, and each meal is a hearty one, as the adults eat insects four or five inches long. They also seem to be immune to the poison of a certain green caterpillar. The slightest touch from one of its venomous spines causes a human intense and long-lasting pain, but the birds crush the bugs in their bills and swallow them without any trouble.

The appetite for caterpillars is one characteristic shared by most cuckoos. In other ways the different members of the family go to all possible extremes of behavior. Some are promiscuous and others mate for the breeding season, while the Squirrel Cuckoos appear to be permanently paired. Nests range from the neat domes of the coucals, through great communal basins and frail platforms, to borrowed ones of other species. Though most parasites desert their young completely, the Didrics feed them, at least. Some chicks are attended by groups of adults, who may be either caring or careless. Others are raised by their own two parents and zealously defended from danger—even from fire, in the case of the White-browed Coucal.

The birds range in length from the six inches of the bright African species to two feet or more for some of the ground dwellers. The behavior of these terrestial ones is far from that of the expert flyers. However, the Madagascar couas, with species that travel both in the air and on the earth, demonstrate how such differences can evolve among relatives.

Still, many cuckoos show surface similarities. People grouped them together, just as they did more obviously connected birds, such as gulls and penguins.

For years these casual classifications were taken for granted. Then, in the nineteenth century, attempts were made to define bird families more scientifically, through morphological studies, based on the dissection of dead specimens.

Details of their internal structure confirmed the relationship between the cuckoos. In all their skulls, certain palate bones were fused together, and another small bone, the vomer, was missing. They also still retained a little leg muscle other species have lost.

Birds rub their bills on oil glands above their tails. Then they can lubricate their plumage while grooming it. Often there are tufts of little feathers above these glands —but not in cuckoos.

More features that set the cuckoos apart are two carotid arteries in their necks rather than only one, dead-end pouches opening off their intestines, like human appendixes, and the zygodactyl feet.

Many bird families show one or more of these characteristics, but only the cuckoos have all of them. The

67

palates of ducks contain fused bones like those of the cuckoos, but their webbed feet are certainly not zygodactyl. And woodpeckers, despite the two-by-two arrangement of their toes, are missing the "caeca"—the pouches in the intestine.

The physical boundaries of the cuckoos were defined long ago. If the anatomy of every known cuckoo could be examined now, new and different standards might have to be set for the family. It is probable that many ornithologists today are no longer familiar with what makes a cuckoo a cuckoo. The classification has become a tradition.

If the hoatzin is formally admitted into the family, the list of cuckoo features will have to be changed. They have vomer bones in their palates and three front toes opposite a single hind one. Dr. Sibley felt that the hoatzins would have been recognized as cuckoos years ago if only their feet had been zygodactyl.

Another question about cuckoos is, simply, how many species are there? Estimates range from 94 to 142. A species is a group of animals changed so much from its fellows that they cannot interbreed. However, it is difficult to trace the family trees of elusive birds. What one scientist considers a species may be reduced to a subspecies by another.

There is much research still to be done. How did cuckoos in widely separated areas evolve similar behavior, like the ground-living ones spread from Asia to America? Why did brood parasitism develop? And how are the birds related? Many questions remain about cuckoos, even though they have fascinated people for centuries and influenced both language and literature.

Coucal

Songs & Superstitions

CUCKOOS & PEOPLE

The cuckoos have many popular names, borrowed from mammals, other birds and reptiles. They are also described by their actions—the roadrunner; their food—Lizard Cuckoo; their size—Greater Coucal; their appearance—Hawk Cuckoo; their range—Indian Cuckoo; their hosts—Drongo Cuckoo; and even their smell—"Stinking Hannah."

Other creatures, in turn, have been named for the cuckoos, including fish, birds, and parasitic insects. Cuckoo eyes, grass, pints, breads, and shoes are all flowers that bloom in the spring when the bird's cry echoes through the woods. "Cuckoo lambs" are born between April and June, while "cuckoo ale" is drunk out of doors to welcome the return of the migrants—and of pleasant weather.

71

But the outstanding features of cuckoos are their calls, which people have imitated in so many ways: cuckoo, coua, coucal, koel. The Spanish translate the sound as "cucú" and the French as "coucou." In far away New Zealand the Maoris dubbed the birds "koekoes," since "kuku" was already assigned to a pigeon. The Greek name, "kokkyx," turned into the term, "coccyx," for the bone at the base of our spines, which is supposedly shaped like a cuckoo's bill.

The birds' songs were even the subject of a "Pogo" cartoon, published in 1952. The pudgy little porcupine questioned a Black-billed Cuckoo about its voice. The bird claimed that "the American way" for a cuckoo to call was to "holler 'Gowk, kulk.' " This saved it from being put to work. Pogo had wanted the Black-bill to take up residence in a clock, like its European relatives, but he changed his mind at the prospect of listening to "Gowk, kulk" twenty-four times a day, or more.

Perhaps the call gets so much attention because the shy birds are easier to find by sound than sight. Their distinctive "cuckoos" proclaimed the arrival of spring, always a welcome message. An English round from about 1300 encouraged the bird's musical efforts. "Summer is acoming in, loud sing, cuckoo! . . . Merry sing, cuckoo, cuckoo."

In even earlier times the bird was recognized as a herald of warm weather. Ancient Greeks listened to it and planned their farming activities.

The Cuckoo Flower blooms when the bird returns to England in the spring.

When the cuckoo sings among the oak trees it is time to plough . . . if it should . . . happen to rain three days together when the cuckoo sings . . . then late sowing will be as good as early.

And, long ago, the English also relied on the bird.

When the cuckoo comes to your bare thorn,
Sell your cow and buy your corn.

In Europe, the cuckoo was an agricultural adviser. Across the ocean the American Rain Crows foretold the weather. Could they know even more about what the future would bring? People thought so for many years and asked the birds how soon they would marry, the number of children they would have, and when they would die. Each "cuckoo" meant a baby, or another year to wait for marriage—or death.

It was a simple step from these superstitions to the belief that the birds could change one's luck for better— or worse. If a cry comes on the first of May from the north, tragedy is sure. The other three directions bring better fortune: south, a rich harvest; west, good luck; and east, success in love.

If you are standing on hard ground when you hear the earliest cuckoo, trouble is on the way, but soft earth predicts a favorable future. This fancy might be based on fact. At planting time in the spring, hospitable fields are better than solidly compacted land.

It is also a hopeful sign to have coins in your pocket while listening to the first song of the season. A wish made while you "turn the money" by jingling it in your pocket is sure to come true. Of course, just having a handful of change might fulfill at least a small wish.

The superstitions, repeated in England and many European countries, have traveled to America. Another folk belief, based on the Common Cuckoo's parasitism, has reached the southern United States, although it is not really appropriate where cuckoos raise their own families. Once people thought a female mated with the male of her chosen host species, not with another cuckoo. The foster mother was treated shabbily twice over. First her mate was stolen, and then she could raise no offspring of her own, only the invading cuckoo chick. So a glimpse of the bird warns that one woman will betray another, and the poor victim can never have children. Since the cuckoo was supposed to trick her mate, too, this idea led to the word, "cuckold," for a man whose wife is unfaithful.

Others envied the male cuckoo, who escaped his responsibilities as husband and father so skillfully. In *The Merry Wives of Windsor*, Shakespeare wrote that, come springtime, "The cuckoo then, on every tree, mocks married men."

The people who worked and walked in the English countryside were shrewd observers of bird behavior. They showed imagination in explaining it. An old children's song suggests that it was the cuckoo's delight in her melodies that left her no time for family life.

> She sucks little birds' eggs
> To make her voice clear,
> That she may sing Cuckoo!
> Three months in the year.

> The cuckoo is a lazy bird,
> She never builds a nest.
> She makes herself busy
> By singing to the rest.

She never hatches her own young,
And that we all know,
But leaves it for some other bird
While she cries "Cuckoo."

The cuckoos of Europe and America were not the only ones to arouse human curiosity—and fantasy. The people of Borneo have an explanation for the coucal's dull colors. It seems that bird and an Argus Pheasant agreed to decorate each other. The talented coucal spent many hours painting the pheasant's wings with colorful patterns like the iridescent eyes on a peacock's tail.

When the task was finished, and it was the coucal's turn, the pheasant proved to be a lazy bird. It screamed that danger was coming and fled, upsetting the paint pots in its haste. Dark black drenched the coucal's body and plain brown stained its wings. And that was all the decoration the patient artist received.

An Indian legend from the American West also explains the roadrunner's typically dull cuckoo plumage. Once it was a bright and beautiful bird, and a helpful one. Some Indians returned from hunting to find their fire turned to ashes. They asked the swift roadrunner to fetch a burning branch from the fire of the lightning god. They knew that this bird could "fold up the earth" with its long strides. They would not have long to wait for heat and light.

But, when the roadrunner reached his mountain home,

the god roared, "No!" Not daunted by the thunderous voice, the wily bird waited until it had a chance to steal a glowing stick from the fire. It curled its tail around the prize and raced away like the wind.

As the lightning god threw flaming bolts after the thief, the roadrunner scooted into the bed of a dry wash for protection. It was safe, but its waving crest was charred into spikes. Its scorched back was brown, and its eyes had grown red from the clouds of smoke. And this is the way roadrunners have looked ever since.

Another legend pictures the roadrunner as one among a variety of birds who lived together like an Indian tribe. Unfortunately it seemed to be the least popular in the group and was never allowed to join the seed-gathering parties. It had trouble finding food to keep itself and its aged mother alive. The gods took pity on the lonely, hungry bird and suggested some tricks which might make it a welcome part of community life. Alas, none of them worked.

In the end, the roadrunner was given zygodactyl feet. The gods reasoned that they would keep hostile birds from following the outcast. Trackers would never know whether it was coming or going.

Roadrunners befuddle their enemies—and much about cuckoos remains a puzzle. But they are certainly birds which have impressed the people whose world they share. Someone unable to tell a pipit from a godwit quickly recognizes the cuckoo's call. The birds have earned their place in human lives and legends, even their reputation for magical powers. We will always be affected by the shy creatures' haunting voices, signs of spring and storm.

> O blithe newcomer! I have heard,
> I hear thee and rejoice;
> O cuckoo! shall I call thee Bird,
> Or but a wandering voice?
>
> Thrice welcome, darling of the Spring!
> Even yet thou are to me
> No bird, but an invisible thing,
> A voice, a mystery.

> —William Wordsworth, *To the Cuckoo*

Appendix

CLASSIFICATION AND CHARACTERISTICS

Kingdom—Animal Phylum—Chordata Class—Aves (Birds)

Sub-family	Genus (Number of species in genus is shown in parentheses)	Species	Common Name
Cuculinae	Cuculus (12)	canorus	European Cuckoo
		varius	Hawk Cuckoo
	Clamator (5)	glandarius	Great Spotted Cuckoo
	Chrysococcyx (4)	caprius	Didric Cuckoo
		cupreus	Emerald Cuckoo
	Chalcites (8)	lucidus	Shining Cuckoo
	Eudynamys (1)	scolopacea	Common Koel
	Surniculus (1)	lugubris	Drongo Cuckoo
Phaenicophaenae	Piaya (5)	cayana	Squirrel Cuckoo
	Coccyzus (8)	americanus	Yellow-billed Cuckoo
		erythropthalmus	Black-billed Cuckoo
	Phaenicophaeus (1)	pyrrhocephalus	Red-faced Malkoha
Crotophaginae	Opisthocomus (1)	hoazin	Hoatzin
	Crotophaga (3)	ani	Smooth-billed Ani
		sulcirostris	Groove-billed Ani
	Guira (1)	guira	Guira
Neomorphinae	Geococcyx (2)	californianus	Greater Roadrunner
Couinae	Coua (10)	delalandei	Delalande's Coua
Centropodinae	Centropus (27)	sinensis	Greater Coucal
		superciliosus	White-browed Coucal

OF THE CUCKOOS IN THE BOOK

Order—Cuculiformes (Cuckoo-shaped)   Family—Cuculidae

Range	Habitat	Nests
Europe Africa Asia	Trees	Parasitic
India to Burma Ceylon	Trees	Parasitic
Africa Near East S. Europe	Trees	Parasitic
Africa	Trees	Parasitic
Africa	Trees	Parasitic
Australia Pacific islands	Trees	Parasitic
Southeast Asia to Australia	Trees	Parasitic
Southeast Asia	Trees	Parasitic
Southern Mexico to Argentina	Trees	Pair
North America winters to Argentina	Trees	Pair
North America winters to Argentina	Trees	Pair
Ceylon	Trees	Pair
South America	Trees	Communal
Southern United States to Argentina	Trees and Ground	Communal and Pair
Southern United States to Argentina	Trees and Ground	Communal and Pair
South America	Trees and Ground	Communal and Pair
Southwest United States Mexico	Ground	Pair
Madagascar	Ground	Pair
Southeast Asia	Trees and Ground	Pair (domed)
East and Central Africa	Trees and Ground	Pair (domed)

Bibliography

A Literary History of England. Edited by Albert C. Baugh. New York: Appleton-Century-Crofts, Inc., 1948.

A New Dictionary of Birds. Edited by Arthur L. Thompson. New York: Thomas Nelson & Sons, 1964.

ARMSTRONG, EDWARD A. *The Folklore of Birds.* New York: Dover Publications, Inc., 1970.
——*The Life and Lore of Birds.* New York: Crown Publishers, Inc., 1975.

BARRUEL, PAUL. *Birds of the World: Their Life and Habits.* New York: Oxford University Press, 1973.

BATES, MARSTON AND THE EDITORS OF *Life. The Land and Wildlife of South America.* New York: Time Incorporated, 1964.

BEEBE, WILLIAM. *Jungle Peace.* New York: Henry Holt & Co., 1918.

BENT, ARTHUR C. *Life Histories of North American Cuckoos, Goatsuckers and their Allies.* Washington: Smithsonian Institution, 1940. New York: Dover Publications, Inc., 1964.

CLEMENT, ROLAND C. *Hammond Nature Atlas of America.* Maplewood, New Jersey: Hammond Incorporated, 1973.

CLEMENTS, J. F. *Birds of the World: A Checklist.* New York: The Two Continents Publishing Company, 1974.

COLBERT, EDWIN H. *Wandering Lands and Animals.* New York: E. P. Dutton & Company, Inc., 1973.

CURRY-LINDAHL, KAI. *Let Them Live: A Worldwide Survey of Animals Threatened with Extinction.* New York: William Morrow & Company, Inc., 1972.

8 2

Bibliography

DAVIS, D. E. "Social Nesting Habits of the *Guira guira.*" *Auk,* 57. Washington: Smithsonian Institution, American Ornithologists Union, 1940.
——"Social Nesting Habits of the Smooth-billed Ani." *Auk,* 57. Washington: Smithsonian Institution, American Ornithologists Union, 1940.

DESMOND, ADRIAN J. *The Hot-blooded Dinosaurs.* New York: The Dial Press, 1976.

DORST, JEAN. *The Life of Birds.* New York: Columbia University Press, 1971.

FISHER, JAMES; AND PETERSON, ROGER TORY. *The World of Birds.* Garden City, New York: Doubleday & Company, Inc., 1964.

FORBUSH, EDWARD H.; AND MAY, JOHN R. *Natural History of the Birds of Eastern and Central North America.* Boston: Houghton Mifflin Company, 1939.

GOODERS, J. *The Great Book of Birds.* New York: The Dial Press, 1975.

GOODWIN, GRENVILLE. *Myths and Tales of the White Mountain Apache.* New York: American Folk-lore Society, 1939. New York: Kraus Reprint, 1969.

GRIMMER, J. LEAR. "Strange Little World of the Hoatzin." *National Geographic Magazine,* 122. Washington: National Geographic Society, 1962.

HARRISON, HAL H. *A Field Guide to Birds' Nests in the United States East of the Mississippi River.* Boston: Houghton Mifflin Company, 1975.

LaRousse Encyclopedia of Animal Life. New York: Hamlyn Publishing Group Limited, 1967.

MACKINNON, JOHN; AND MACKINNON, KATHLEEN. *Animals of Asia: the Ecology of the Oriental Region.* New York: Holt, Rinehart & Winston, 1974.

OLIVERAS, ANTONIO; AND MUNVES, J. A. "Predatory Behavior of the Smooth-billed Ani." *Auk,* 90. Washington: Smithsonian Institution, American Ornithologist Union, 1973.

ORR, ROBERT T. *The Animal Kingdom.* New York: The Macmillan Company, 1965.

Bibliography

Our Magnificent Wildlife. Pleasantville, New York: Reader's Digest Association, Inc., 1975.

PETERSON, ROGER TORY. *A Field Guide to the Birds.* Boston: Houghton Mifflin Company, 1947.
——*A Field Guide to Western Birds.* Boston: Houghton Mifflin Company, 1941.
——AND THE EDITORS OF *Life. The Birds.* New York: Time Incorporated, 1963.

POTTER, STEPHEN; AND SARGENT, LAURENS. *Pedigree: the Origin of Words from Nature.* New York: Taplinger Publishing Company, 1973.

ROTHSCHILD, MIRIAM; AND CLAY, THERESA. *Fleas, Flukes and Cuckoos.* New York: The Philosophical Library, Inc., 1952.

SHAW, ANNA MOORE. *Pima Indian Legends.* Tuscon: University of Arizona Press, 1968.

SHORT, LESTER L. *Birds of the World.* New York: Grosset & Dunlap, 1975.

SIBLEY, CHARLES G.; AND AHLQUIST, JON E. "The Relationships of the Hoatzin." *Auk*, 90. Washington: Smithsonian Institution, American Ornithologists Union, 1973.

SKUTCH, ALEXANDER F. *Parent Birds and Their Young.* Austin: University of Texas Press, 1976.

The Oxford Dictionary of Nursery Rhymes. Edited by Iona Opie and Peter Opie. London: Oxford University Press, 1952.

The World of Birds. Edited by John Honders. New York: Peebles Press, 1975.

TINBERGEN, NIKO; AND THE EDITORS OF *Life. Animal Behavior.* New York: Time Incorporated, 1965.

WELTY, JOEL. *The Life of Birds.* Philadelphia: W. B. Saunders Co., 1975.

WING, L. W. *Natural History of Birds.* New York: The Ronald Press Company, 1956.

World Atlas of Birds. Edited by Peter M. Scott. New York: Random House, Inc., 1974.

Index

Italic numbers refer to illustrations